HOW TO THINK LIKE A MILLIONAIRE
TIPS AND TRICKS TO BE MORE PRODUCTIVE AND MAKE BIG MONEY

PHIL JOHNSON

I0484813

Copyright © 2015 by D/O Publishing

Introduction

People always have three wishes, just in case a genie in a bottle comes rolling down their way. The first in the list is almost always "to become rich". The second is to be "successful". The third is hit and miss; it could be fame, love, peace of mind, or something about their health.

All those things mentioned are beautiful. But let's be honest, you would like to be rich and successful as well. After all, what bad will come out of it? Being rich means you can buy whatever you like, go wherever you desire, do whatever you want to do. Being successful means people will look up to you. It means you will have the power to inspire them. It means you will be capable of changing their life as well, for the better.

Since these goals are big and it seem like they cannot wait, we tend to rush on things. We invest on businesses we don't know anything about. We connect with and try to impress people we do not even like. We spend money, time, and effort on things that we "think" will make us rich and successful. But we fail to look into ourselves.

I have to be honest with you. This book is not filled with money making tips for your online business. It does not even have statistics or stratagems on which businesses are profitable. What it has is something more rewarding in the long run.

It will help you become a better person.

It will tackle 8 aspects in our life and how we can face them with strength and grace. Each section will be accompanied by quotes from some of the world's most renowned personalities: allowing us to have a brief look on what they think.

If you're ready to start this journey, I invite you to turn to the next page.

Friendship

"Lots of people want to ride with you in the limo, but what you want is someone who will take the bus with you when the limo breaks down."
-Oprah Winfrey

We all know how important it is to have people in our lives that support, care about and build us up. Be it family members, good old friends, work colleagues or business partners, these people should be on our side *at all times*, helping us face every obstacle that might come into our lives. Not that they will be "spoiling" us, but they should be eager to make us become a better person.

Sometimes though, things might get difficult and people might start working against – rather than with us. This is what we should all keep in mind when it comes to the friendships we have and how they can help us improve and become better persons:

Don't trust everybody

As counter-intuitive as it might sound, keeping those who doesn't seem trustworthy at a distance can be extremely beneficial in the long run. Not everyone is going to like you, and that is completely okay, so be aware of those who might want to make you trip and fall on your way to success. Be kind and honest, but don't just trust anyone who comes your way *even* if he or she shows up with good demeanor. There are many ways to spot the fake "friends". Body language, the way they talk, their eyes, or simply your gut feeling. Be vigilant.

Take the time to know someone

A strong, meaningful friendship is hard to achieve, that's why you should put up the work and effort into it, especially if it seems beneficial for both of you. A good, real friend who believes in you and your abilities can help you see the good in yourself, also, pushing you to improve and become an overall better human being.

Surrounding yourself with the "right" people

Start surrounding yourself with cheerful, positive and successful people as much as you can, for you terd to follow their habits and ways of thinking. Look up to people you admire and try to do what they do: but in your own, unique way. Don't be afraid to put yourself out there: get noticed and speak up your mind in corporate or high-class circles. Success has boldness and courage in it.

Show your helping side

If you can, help someone. You'll never know when you might need a helping hand, so building powerful, positive connections is extremely important. Be a person who can be trusted, so you can create a strong and secure circle of friends and acquaintances that you can rely on in times of need. This is not a form of trickery, but rather, this is a way of attracting people who are more likely to help you too, in the future.

Network and Connect

Go out to meetings, attend various lectures and seminars held by famous people, go to exhibitions and events – in a word, network. Connect with those you respect and admire, but be careful to not lose yourself on the way up.

ACTION PLAN:

Reflect and see who your friends are. Are they really "friends", or are they just wolves in sheep's clothing? Once you have identified those who are more likely to bring you down rather than lift you up, stay away from them, little by little.

As for your REAL friends, take care of them. Spend more time with them and strengthen your bond.

Having good friends is of utmost importance when it comes to attaining a wealthy, prosperous way of life. Developing healthy, beneficial connections with those who might help you is a good thing, but don't neglect your old friends, either. Remember that if your friends are real, they will be there for you through thick or thin.

Improvement

"Your most unhappy customers are your greatest source of learning."
-Bill Gates

We all love praises. We love it when we are being applauded for what we did. We love to be recognized for something we poured our efforts to. We feed on the happy comments and the acknowledgements.

There is nothing wrong with that. After all, praises, recognitions, and acknowledgements keep us inspired. BUT once we stagnate with them, we'll start to fall down. When we let all the good things get in our head, we'll refuse to grow and improve. As our competitors seek to become better, we get stunted.

In any business or career, you should ALWAYS welcome feedbacks: both good and bad.

More than just a suggestion box

Your business will not be successful if all you will do is submerge yourself in all the positive feedbacks that you are receiving. What you need to do is listen to those who are not happy with the service you are providing them. Hand out survey forms and feedback mechanism and filter those who have honest reviews. Listen to them because it's one proven way to get better in your craft.

Just because you have a suggestion box lying in the corner, doesn't mean that people will take the effort to use it. You have to initiate the move. Make it easier for them to leave their comments.

Same goes for career. Don't wait for your boss' comments-- eagerly ask him for it!

There IS a solution

Once the bad comments are in, you will know what the problems are. No matter how big it is, there is always a solution around the corner. Never tell anyone that "you cannot do anything about it". That's equivalent to business/career suicide.

The only thing you have to do is keep a clear head, have a broad vision of the bigger picture and train your mind to remain open to alternatives. Having to face a setback, be it in your personal life or in your career, might help you shift your perspectives to the better roads, since it can give you clue and facts regarding your current status.

Ask your clients or customers. Ask your employees. Ask your boss for an advice. What can solve the current problem? Whatever you do, don't tell yourself that you are doomed. A solution is lying there somewhere, you just have to find it.

Be consistent in improvement

Give a clear and honest thought on what happened, focusing on the causes of the problem; and then start working on building yourself (or your business) while having the right solutions in mind. Constant self development is a powerful tool in creating and becoming your best self, therefore you should make this your full-time activity. Real, powerful improvement takes time and a couple of huge mistakes– that's why you should make a constant effort to invest wisely in your self-developments and financial well-being.

ACTION PLAN:

There are many ways to improve your career or business. One of them is turning your weaknesses into strengths. Start TODAY. List down things that you NEED to improve and work on them one at a time.

Survey forms are great for customers-- give them freebies for answering it honestly. Consider this as a form of investment. When your clients realize that you want things to be better for them, they will patronize you more! And you'll earn not just money, but loyalty! Sit down with your employees. Talk to them about improvement. When they recognize your will to make things better for them, they'll work hard and be more productive. Ask your boss, if you do, he'll know that you are eager for knowledge.

It can even apply to your personal like. Communicate with your kids, with your spouse, with your friends. Ask them what can be improved to make your relationships more fulfilling.

Unhappy and unsatisfied clients, just as problems and mistakes, can happen to everyone. Although this might feel like a setback at first, having the right attitude matters a great deal! Only then you can clearly see the faults that have been made and what caused them to happen. On the way, you will also see the right solutions. All of these help in bringing about that well-desired improvement, in both personal and professional life.

Savings

"I think that much of the advice given to young men about saving money is wrong. I never saved a cent until I was forty years old. I invested in myself – in study, in mastering my tools, in preparation. Many a man who is putting a few dollars a week into the bank would do much better to put it into himself."
-Henry Ford of Ford Motors

Saving money is believed to be, from early ages, of high importance in everybody's lives. Be it education, retirement money or investing into a business, more and more people find themselves conditioned to save money. In some cases, this might be a very healthy, very rational approach, but it can very well become a factor for stagnation and torpidity.

Of course, a good investment always pays off in the long run, but to truly and effectively succeed in life, one should keep min mind that it's not all about savings.

Choose to invest in yourself

Having an academic education is, of course, important, but you have to ask yourself first it that is what you want. If it isn't, then why spend money for it? A healthier approach is to find something you really enjoy and begin investing in it. No matter what it is, be it painting, programming or car mechanics, choosing to invest in a **passion** will not only bring you satisfaction, but it will also make you a great candidate on the marketplace.

The value of experience

Time is money, that's why you should be careful on what you're filling it with. Experience, in this case, has been proven to be of much more relevance in the long run, rather than accumulating lots of so-called facts which will only stay in the head for quite some time. Don't be greedy with education alone! Invest money for your experience!

Indulge NOW

Do whatever it takes to get yourself where you want to be, making sure you put your money to good use. Saving your income into a bank account for later might seem like a good idea, but you would be much better off if you start using them on things that matter to you now. Spending should not always be geared on self improvement or education. It can also be spent on things that you love. Reward yourself!

What will you do with the money when you are already old? When you can no longer travel? When you no longer have the use for shopping all out? Reward yourself from time to time!

ACTION PLAN:

Divide your income or revenue accordingly using the following formula:

30% should be for your savings. Henry Ford's quote is quite extreme. His time before is different in our time now. Have savings for your old age, or for emergencies, and for your kids. A part of it can even be used to invest in a new business, or to improve your current business!

50% can be used for your expenses: utilities in the house, rent, maintenance medications and food. If you have a partner in life, you can lower down this percentage.

10% should be saved for your learning. Whatever that learning may be. It can be spent to improve your current craft. It can also be spent to learn a new craft. As long as you expanding in terms of knowledge and experience, this money is well-spent!

10% should be for leisure. Buy yourself new shoes. Or go watch a concert. Get a well-deserved massage.

Please note that this is just a sample formula. You can tailor it according to your needs and wants. If you are leaning on buying a new car, then include that in your budget!

Choosing to invest your income into something meaningful, as well as using your money to grow and master a certain passion or a skill can be extremely rewarding and relevant if you want to become a rich and successful individual. It's much more important to grow yourself, rather than a bank account.

Ventures

"The biggest risk is not taking any risk... In a world that's changing really quickly, the only strategy that is guaranteed to fail is not taking risks."
-Mark Zuckerberg of Facebook

In both personal and professional life, we are sometimes put to face hard, tough decisions; some of them are even life-changing. Since we are afraid of change, we tend to choose the decision that will maintain the status quo. Why? Because it is safe, because by doing that, we don't need to worry about the uncertainties the change may bring.

The thing is, if we always turn our backs on risks, we risk being left behind.

Start now

You might feel discouraged, you might feel that you're unprepared or you might feel like you're going to fail. Don't. Now is a good time as any, so ditch the waiting game. Take all of the chances and opportunities you can get and start doing it now. Waiting for a perfect moment that might (or might not) occur later in life can be disastrous to yourself and your business, so just start.

Dare to be bold

If you have an idea for a business, go with it at full-force. Trust your abilities and skills and don't worry too much about the outcome. Instead, focus on learning as you go at your own pace, all the while taking **conscious** risks. It pays off much more than constant planning, especially if all those plans will forever remain as plans and not one action will be performed.

It does not mean though, that you will be reckless. While taking the risk, you also have to be careful. If the risk turned out to be a wrong move, well, at least you've learned. That's better than constantly thinking about "what if's"...

ACTION PLAN:

Do you have a business in mind? That one business that you would really like to do, but can't seem to start with? Do you have the starting capital for it? If you don't, then begin earning, but don't put the plan off JUST BECAUSE you still do not have enough capital for it. Once you have enough to start, then start!

Read business resources online. Begin planning. Take ONE HOUR each day to plan and when it's all set, take two-three hours of your day to handle your business. This is especially good if the business you have in mind can be achieved online.

Do you plan to be promoted? If you are, start expanding your skills and knowledge by investing in yourself.

The bottom line is this: do not be afraid of change. You cannot expect things to be different when what you are doing is similar to what you've done before.

Success is not all about rigorous planning, but also about an individual sense of adventure and playfulness. If you're willing to get yourself out there and try as many things as you want, you will eventually become more fulfilled, more satisfied and more prosperous. Letting yourself risk can be a sure way path to success!

Fate

"Everybody is a genius. But if you judge a fish by its ability to climb a tree, it will live its whole life believing that it is stupid."
-Albert Einstein

The standards we set for ourselves can sometimes be a little bit harsh, especially if we struggle to achieve great accomplishments in both our personal and professional life. Sometimes, having ***unrealistic goals*** and expectations can be delusional and also self-destructive, so we should all learn to look inside ourselves, listen to our utmost desires and then have the courage to pursue our true, authentic passions.

Don't be unfair

Before you reprimand yourself for not being good at your current craft, did you take the time to analyze if that craft is really what you want to do? Don't be unfair. How can you expect to be good at something you don't even like? If you constantly feel stressed and tired, perhaps now is a good time to reflect. Are you fulfilling your purpose?

Find your calling

Take your time to sit with yourself and find what it is you like, what excites your spirit and what makes you honestly and genuinely happy. In order for that to happen, you must go out and do stuff, get involved in as many activities as you can and connect with others, until you find something in which you're naturally good at. This might take a while, but don't get discouraged, everybody – including you – is instinctively skilled at at least one thing.

Follow your dreams

If you still remember what you used to dream about when you were a kid or a teenager, no matter how absurd it may have seemed, that's probably what your true self desires. Don't become rigid: always thinking that the only way to success is to climb the corporate ladder. Once you have reunited with your dreams, be bold enough to follow them, and do what you have to do to achieve your goals. There is nothing more satisfying than doing what you were truly meant to do.

Set realistic goals

Try to have the bigger picture in mind at all times, but also learn to develop a strategic plan on how to get there. Take it one step at a time because turning a passion into a sustaining career usually takes a lot of energy, diligence and determination. Having a structured plan in mind – and on paper - is the key to become a successful, thriving and fruitful person.

Don't start a business now and expect to be rich after one month! When your time is up and you're still not rich, you will feel discouraged! And then what will you do? Ditch your dream because nothing came out of it? Wrong approach.

Set realistic goals along with your plans. That way, each little achievement will be a form of fuel: motivating you to go ahead.

Keep going

Success is not always guaranteed, but it **can** be achieved. If you face challenges and obstacles along your way, the goal is to not get discouraged, but rather learn from the mistakes, and then continue. Remember: this is your passion; you have already concluded that it is what you want and what you are good at. A few glitches on the road should not stop you from achieving your goals!

ACTION PLAN:

You decide on what your fate is going to be. Don't let the people around you dictate you on it. Don't let the standards set by the community force their fates on you.

Start today. Do you want to do things differently? What's stopping you from choosing your ways? Reflect and you will soon realize that YOU are stopping yourself. Just because people around you have the same approach to things, does not mean that you have to be one of them. Dare to be different. When you do things according to your own ways, you'll notice that you are more productive, and hence, you'll have more chances to be successful.

Is your job your calling? If it isn't then start planning now to shift your career.

Everyone has the capacity to become a better, more successful individual, and as Albert Einstein said, everyone has the seed of genius rooted inside them. We have to be courageous enough to find that genius and then excel at it, as we all have our place in the world.

Leadership

"My job is not to be easy on people. My job is to make them better."
-Steve Jobs of Apple

A good, powerful leader is one that influences, inspires and makes people want to improve themselves, becoming better individuals. Anyone can be a leader; he doesn't have to be a CEO, a manager or a business owner. Anyone with the willingness to inspire others can become a hero for somebody else, aiding them on the way to success and fortune.

Positive leadership, however, requires a high dose of diligence, patience, and a strong sense of individuality, as well as the ability to feel others' needs and aspirations. By following a set of guidelines, anyone can start improving their leadership skills:

Know yourself

To be a good leader, one must first master his or her own self. Knowing what you truly like or dislike, what your passions and dreams are and what makes you who you are - all great assets for a future great leader.

Be one that inspires

Don't tell people what to do. Rather, encourage them by doing what needs to be done, by stepping up and showing them how it should be done. Don't expect immediate results, either. Good outcomes come in time, and a true leader should know this by heart. This is what real entrepreneurs do: they set a standard, and then they encourage people to achieve that standard by constantly growing. This is a surefire sign that you're being a good leader for your team.

Use the power of example

An exceptional leader will invite people to follow his or her example, rather than chase endless lists or useless advice. Setting the right tone for your employees, clients or anyone, in general, is one great and secure way of getting the most out of those around you. If, for example, you want them to be more positive, focused and result-oriented, you begin by being like that yourself, so that they could have a clear guideline to follow and adopt.

Be a good communicator

Communication is essential in everything: be it a circle of close friends, a family, a small business or a large organization. Good communication skills are highly recommended for a capable and influential leader, for he or she must know how to talk and encourage people in various ways. A powerful, uplifting speech or an inspiring pep talk can be as beneficial to the people as it is for the leader, helping them all in building themselves.

Learn from EVERYONE

As a great leader, you shouldn't get stagnant in your endeavor to become successful, wealthy and fulfilled. Continuous learning is an important aspect for everyone. Learn from everywhere: from your colleagues, your friends, your employees, even from those you don't particularly like, since everyone holds great lessons and significant advice.

Don't lose yourself

Even if you're a leader of a prestigious company, you should not forget one important aspect: don't turn yourself into a lofty, unreachable person. Remain simple and humble, so you can appear as a loving, compassionate person who would help people if they would ever need it. It might appear a little counter-productive, but keeping a dose of humility can help you improve from within. Both your employees and your clients will appreciate and respect you more, as their mentor as well as a friend.

Be hard when needed

You cannot spoon-feed your people. You cannot always talk to them like they are a child who needs infinite amount of patience. You also have to be hard and punishing with them if the situation calls for it, especially if they are not showing any sign of repentance or desire for improvement.

ACTION PLAN:

There are three fundamental things you have to keep in mind if you want to be a leader.

1. Send feedbacks
2. Be friendly...
3. But stay professional

The first make your business or career improve. The second will urge people to talk to you in times on need, and the third will give you an authoritative air- subtly telling people that they have to follow you.

One of the greatest, most successful leaders of this world, Apple's founder Steve Jobs believed that a great leader is not one who dictates and gives advice, but rather one who builds and nurtures, inspiring people to improve in their own ways.

Teamwork

"Talent wins games, but teamwork and intelligence wins championships."
- Michael Jordan

For any business, company or institution to function at its best, you have to invest on people. Investing in real, powerful work relations is an effective way to turn your business from a simple and dull workplace into a fruitful and emerging community. In order to achieve that higher degree of functionality for your business, enforcing teamwork into the social environment is crucial.

Being one of the most important tools in building and sustaining a trade or a business, teamwork gets more and more recognition and value now. Any company manager or business owner should know how to implement teamwork in their workplaces, especially since most of the tips are quite simple and can be of good use to anyone:

Create a powerful vision
When your business or company has a great, meaningful vision, it will draw towards it the right people – individuals that will diligently and enthusiastically work together to see that vision materialized. Also, knowing that the object of work - whatever it might be - is purposeful and relevant, would greatly empower people to give their best: doing their jobs properly and well. The certainty that your work matters and it contributes to the well-being of the world really ties teams together for longer.

Let your people be friends
Consider boosting your employees' working attitude by encouraging them to engage in various activities and tasks that might help them become closer to each other, finding common passions, hobbies and personality traits. This help to promote a healthier, more diversified workplace, whereas teamwork plays an essential role.

Open channels for dialogue
An easy, smooth communication flow in a company is extremely important, that is why every manager or business owner should take into consideration the improvement of this area. A workplace where people talk to each other, expressing their thoughts and opinions, will help solve any given task more

effectively. Good communication, both internal and external, is a key element when it comes to building a good foundation for your business. It's extremely important for an organization to provide counselling and advice to their employees.

Appreciate and respect

For teamwork to be practical and potent inside an organization, a good manager would try to see the worth in every employee and will inspire others to do the same among their circles. Appreciation bolsters a sense of achievement and worth, both of these things being mandatory in a strong, secure and stable community. A reliable team works better than one individual, since members can help and sustain each other when it's needed.

Spread enthusiasm

A cheerful, enthusiastic mood is contagious, so go ahead and share your passion for your business with everyone you work it. This will instantly create a sense of belonging, as well as it will help building better, more secure connections between people in your organization. An optimistic manner would help motivate and excite your team, propelling them in the right direction.

Provide feedback

Your team members should know whether or not they're doing a good job, so they could improve and advance in the future. Always make sure that their tasks get recognized and acknowledged, encouraging them to ask for guidelines and advice in case they face difficulties or any other type of trouble. Pay attention to everyone's needs and wishes and try, as much as you can, to respond to them with care.

ACTION PLAN:

Organize monthly team building events. They do not have to be grand. Even a simple get together with games and a few inspirational talks will go a long way. From time to time, send your employees to seminars, so that they will be better in honing their skills. Always remind them of the company's vision. Encourage all of them to become leaders on their own by having projects where each one must act as the leader.

You business is not just a money-making machine. If it delivers happiness to employees, they will treat it as home. When they do, they will become more lucrative in their work.

Teamwork, as the name suggests, is what makes a team work. Michael Jordan, the great basketball player once said that a powerful sense of community matters more than individual work, since two – or more people think better than one.

Failure

"Optimism is a perfectly legitimate response to failure."
– Stephen King

We all know how important it is to always keep a positive, optimistic attitude, especially in trying times, for they can completely alter a situation and our views regarding it. No matter how dark and bleak a situation may appear, there is always a solution somewhere, and being naturally optimistic can help us find it faster and more effective.

Failure can happen to anyone, but what truly differentiate the real, authentic winners from the rest is having the ability to rise up, learn from mistakes and have the courage to go on, knowing that it can and it will get better. Following some simple, yet powerful steps in achieving that attitude is a surefire way in becoming more positive and thus, more successful:

Failing is not final

Sometimes, a career, a business or a profession can go wrong, and it might not even be your own fault. In times like these, an essential thing is *to not become desperate* about the thought of escape, ding that will make you lose your vision and focus. Instead, try to keep your eyes on the bigger picture, having the certainty that failing at a certain point is just part of the process. Choosing to learn from what happened and applying the lessons in the future is only going to aid you in becoming more successful.

See the good in it

There is always some kind of goodness hiding in even the darkest places, so choosing to focus on them rather than mourning over the past is crucial to becoming a more cheerful and happier person. Having a positive outlook on life - even if you face some hard challenges – can only make you better, regardless of the field you work in.

Be confident

Know that every breakdown is eventually going to pass, for nothing is permanent, not even failure. If you have the boldness and confidence to believe in yourself and your ability to get through defeat, you will succeed at rising-- even higher than you originally thought you can. Success is made of small victories and also some setbacks so don't get discouraged, depressed or pessimistic about it. Be confident enough to try again until it is done.

Give it one, two, three more tries

Being persevering and determined to win is way more important than failing. Trying again means you're *strong and tenacious*, and keeping a winning attitude is going to help you big time along the way. Don't become stagnant, being too quick to give up on your dreams.

Be balanced

Being positive is not about turning yourself into a delusional person, thinking that nothing bad ever happens, it's quite the opposite, actually. It's about taking a responsible and deliberate choice that you will search for a good, suitable solution to whatever hindrance you're facing.

ACTION PLAN:

Nothing needs to be done here except to NEVER GIVE UP. When people tell you that you have failed a hundred times before you became successful, tell them they are wrong. What happened is this: you found a hundred different ways to become successful.

Just as Stephen King says, it's not failure that makes us lose, but rather our attitude towards it. If we choose to see the positive aspects in any situation, no matter how bad it may seem, we will soon enough find the right solution to any problem.

Conclusion

Thanks a lot for downloading this book and I hope it was able to give you a more positive outlook in life.

Remember that no success will ever come to someone who has no clear vision of what he or she wants to have. Success in all endeavors will start within you.

It is important to surround yourself with the right people, that you have the right motivation, the tenacity, and the will to risk. It is also crucial that you learn from mistakes and never give up.

Congratulations on finishing this journey and I hope this book inspired you to become better first. After all, that's the first way to become rich and successful.

Please give us a review if you enjoyed this book. Your positive reviews only help us to make even more informative books!

Check out these other books brought to you by D/O PUBLISHING!

http://www.amazon.com/dp/B00U2WP4H0

STAY HUMAN: THE 8 STEPS TO BECOMING A SALES ROCKSTAR by **Phil Johnson**

STAY HUMAN: THE 8 STEPS TO BECOMING A SALES ROCKSTAR is a fantastic guide that will give you the tools you need to get started as a sales person

Are you new to sales? Are you having trouble hitting sales goal or making connections with your customers? You're not alone. There are a lot of sales people out there but for every good salesman there is, there 9 others that aren't. You don't have to be a part of that unskilled pool of talent.

In this book we'll go through 8 steps that will help analyze your interactions, give you tips and exercises to practice so that you'll be a top ranked salesperson in no time!

STAY HUMAN
The book focuses on taking the emphasis off selling a product and focusing on being genuine to build a connection

HOW TO NAVIGATE INTERACTIONS
We go through everything from the first impression to the final goodbye, setting you up for the best success!

DIFFERENT SCENARIOS
We break down different types of interactions and point at what to look for.

If you're just getting started, or need a fresher in the most practical sales techniques, look no further than STAY HUMAN: THE 8 STEPS TO BECOMING A SALES ROCKSTAR

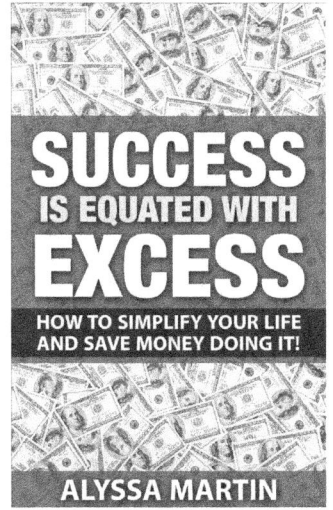

http://www.amazon.com/dp/B00U3H5FNW

SUCCESS IS EQUATED WITH EXCESS: HOW TO SIMPLIFY YOUR LIFE AND SAVE MONEY DOING IT! By **Alyssa Martin**

This guide is for anybody whose trying to declutter their life, find ways to save money and get creative!

ELIMINATE CLUTTER AROUND THE HOUSE
Find effective ways to clean, organize and donate to your local Good Will

GO GREEN
Find different ways to recycle and save power.

FIX YOUR WALLET
Find effective ways to budget your money, organize bills and strategies to save money while shopping!

DO-IT-YOURSELF
Get ideas to create things by your own hand... and save a little money doing it!

http://www.amazon.com/dp/B00U5QA88S

WAKE UP AND GO! A GUIDE TO GET YOUR LIFE BACK by **Matthew Newton**

WAKE UP AND GO! A GUIDE TO GET YOUR LIFE BACK is all in the title. Are you caught in a rut? Feel like you're going in circles and never seem to find happiness? In this guide, we will break down whats pulling you down, and find new ways to rebuild yourself!

LOOK AT YOUR LIFE
We will analyze what's right in wrong at this current moment in time

LOOK AT YOUR LOVE LIFE
Whether you're in a relationship or not, we will get down to the fundamentals and find ways to revitalize your love life!

WHO DO YOU WANT TO BE?
We will take a look at all things that you dreamed of being but used excuses to avoid trying for.

DISCONNECT AND RECONNECT
We will cut ties with the ones the bring us down and we'll give you tips to reconnect with the "friends for a lifetime"

CAREER
We will analyze your job and career ambitions and find ways to improve them or start over all together!

STOP BUYING POSSESSIONS... MAKE MEMORIES
Instead of spending countless dollars on things that will ultimately never be used or break, we find a way to plan a trip of a life time.

AND SO MUCH MORE...

If you need help or guidance on what to do, read this book, do the exercises, and get your life back!

www.ingramcontent.com/pod-product-compliance
Lightning Source LLC
Chambersburg PA
CBHW072253200526
45168CB00015B/1721